Contents

Any words appearing in the text in bold, **like this**, are explained in the Glossary.

Transportation through time

Transport has changed the world. In fact, transport is *continuing* to change the world. Hundreds of years ago, an average person might never travel more than 10 to 15 kilometres or about 6 to 10 miles from where they were born. They would live their whole life in one place, never needing to go anywhere else.

Early forms of transport

In those early years our legs were our only form of transport. Over time, we developed other forms of transport. We rode on animals, or we trained them to pull things such as carts or sledges.

We also began to make use of rivers, by creating the means to float on water. Some civilizations even built their own "rivers" to get around on. Today we call these canals. Once people built bigger boats and used sails, they began to cross oceans and discover entirely new continents.

People began to realize that better and faster transport made the world a smaller place. It may have still taken months or even years to get from one place to another, but at least people were getting there.

Transport is responsible for bringing the different cultures of the world closer together. Without transport, we would not have today's "global community".

THE CUTTING EDGE

TRANSPORTATION

High Speed, Power, and Performance

Mark Morris

Heinemann
LIBRARY

www.heinemann.co.uk/library
Visit our website to find out more information about **Heinemann Library** books.

To order:
☎ Phone 44 (0) 1865 888066
▤ Send a fax to 44 (0) 1865 314091
▢ Visit the Heinemann Bookshop at **www.heinemann.co.uk/library** to browse our catalogue and order online.

First published in Great Britain by Heinemann Library, Halley Court, Jordan Hill, Oxford OX2 8EJ, part of Harcourt Education.
Heinemann is a registered trademark of Harcourt Education Ltd.

Editorial: Sarah Shannon and Kate Bellamy
Design: Richard Parker and Tinstar Design www.tinstar.co.uk
Illustrations: Jeff Edwards
Picture Research: Natalie Gray and Bea Ray
Production: Chloe Bloom

Originated by Digital Imaging
Printed and bound in China by South China Printing Company

ISBN 0 431 13264 X   (hardback)
10 09 08 07 06
10 9 8 7 6 5 4 3 2 1

British Library Cataloguing in Publication Data
Morris, Mark
Transportation (The Cutting Edge)
388
A full catalogue record for this book is available from the British Library.

// MAR 2007

Acknowledgements
The publishers would like to thank the following for permission to reproduce photographs: Alamy p. **15**; Autoexpress pp. **5, 31**; Boeing p. **11**; Corbis pp. **5, 4, 28, 43, 44, 50/51**; Deep Angel p. **13**; Empics pp. **4, 9, 17, 47**; Fountain Power Boats p. **7**; Getty pp. **5, 18/19, 24/25, 29, 30, 39**; GM Autonomy pp. **5, 36**; Honda pp. **4, 26**; NASA pp. **5, 49**; OSF p. **52**; Rex p. **42**; The Air Car pp. **5, 35**; Three Cross Motorcyles pp. **4, 23**; Tramontana Group pp. **4, 32/33**; TRH pp. **38, 46**; US Submarines pp. **4, 6**;

Cover photograph of the Maglev ultra high speed train, reproduced with permission of Hashimoto Noboru/Corbis.

Our thanks to Ian Graham for his assistance in the preparation of this book.

Rapid progress

During the last few centuries, things have changed dramatically. Important inventions such as the steam engine, the aircraft, the jet engine, and the computer have created rapid progress in transport.

The last 100 years in particular have witnessed some amazing changes. Imagine a young girl living in 1903, the same year as the first aeroplane took to the air. That same person would also witness rockets travelling to the Moon just as she was reaching retirement age! That is pretty impressive for a single lifetime.

Journeys that once took months now take hours. And things are likely to get even quicker. But this progress has not been without cost, particularly to the environment. In today's world we do need to get around quickly and cheaply. But scientists are increasingly investigating methods of transportation that do not cause so much pollution.

We have come to rely on transport enormously. Cutting-edge design technology is improving it all the time. But we must be careful it does not cost the Earth.

Best boats

Super speedboats

Cutting-edge ship technology comes with a high price. Speed boats and yachts have always been toys for the very rich.

Phoenix 1000

The Phoenix 1000 is a fantastic new concept. Not only is it a super-yacht with the most luxurious interior you could imagine, it is also a submarine. At the touch of a button you could swap the sunshine and clear blue skies for fascinating and beautiful underwater scenery.

The Phoenix 1000 has two decks. It is incredibly luxurious, with a sauna, jacuzzi, and even a gymnasium. It can easily cross any ocean and it can stay underwater for up to 30 days.

Unfortunately, a luxury craft such as this will cost around US$80 million. The good news is that there is a smaller, cheaper version. The Seattle 1000 still has every possible comfort and luxury, but it is only 36 metres (118 feet) long and only costs around US$20 million!

Phoenix 1000

Length:	65 metres (m) (213 feet)
Width:	8 m (26 feet)
Weight:	1360 tonnes (1500 tons)
Maximum surface speed:	17 **knots**
Maximum submerged speed:	10 knots

The Phoenix 1000 will be the ultimate in luxury at sea – and under it!

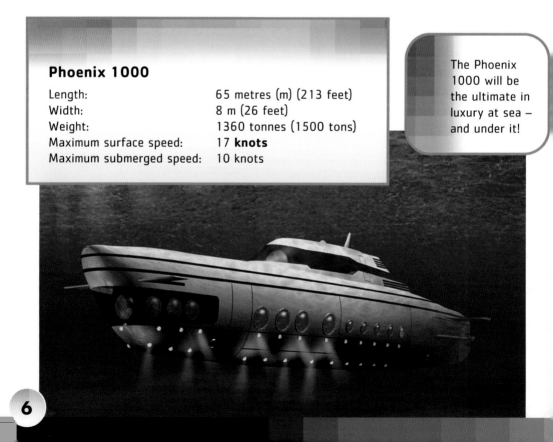

Engineers create **hulls** for powerboats that rise up on top of the water at high speeds. Powerboats skim the surface with very little **drag** to slow them down.

Fountain powerboats

A **powerboat** is an incredibly quick way to cross water, but these boats are not comfortable and are very cramped. They are deafeningly loud and can be highly dangerous. To protect themselves, the crew ride in a cockpit as strong as those on a fighter jet! Powerboats are all about high speed.

Fountain powerboats are some of the fastest, record-breaking boats. As there are many different types of powerboat, there are many different speed records. Fountain boats hold many of these records, including the overall speed record.

In 2004, a Fountain powerboat lifted the overall speed record for **V-hull** boats to over 274 km/h (170 mph). If you want to win races or just make a big show and impress your friends, the record books show that Fountain boats are the first choice.

Hydrofoil power

A hydrofoil is a boat that travels on **foils** with its main hull out of the water. A foil is simply an aircraft wing attached underneath a ship. When the ship picks up speed, the wing creates **lift**, pushing the main hull up out of the water.

This means a hydrofoil travels much faster than ordinary boats. This is because the foils are much smaller than the hull, so less drag is created.

The fastest ferries in the world are hydrofoils. Some are even powered by jet engines that suck in water and then blast it out behind the boat.

Unfortunately there is a maximum size for hydrofoils for them to be practical. Simply building a huge hydrofoil would not work. A bigger foil will increase the amount of lift, but the increased size also means increased weight. These increases cancel each other out. Hydrofoils are only able to carry people. Much bigger cargo ships or huge oil tankers are unable to use hydrofoil technology and so travel much more slowly. Scientists are still working on ways to solve this problem.

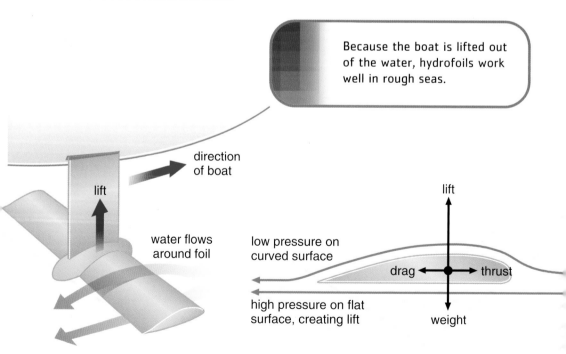

Because the boat is lifted out of the water, hydrofoils work well in rough seas.

direction of boat

lift

water flows around foil

low pressure on curved surface

high pressure on flat surface, creating lift

lift

drag ← → thrust

weight

Cat-link V

A hydrofoil holds the record for the fastest crossing of the North Atlantic Sea. This is the Danish super-ferry, *Cat-link V*. The record is given to the ship that maintains the fastest average speed over the journey.

Cat-link V was the first ship to break the 40-knot barrier. It smashed the record with an average speed of 41.3 knots (76.5 kilometres an hour or 47 miles per hour). Amazingly, *Cat-link V* was delayed for two hours during the record attempt as it took part in a search-and-rescue operation. It also had to cope with rough seas and poor conditions, but it still destroyed the previous record.

Cat-link V not only possesses the cutting-edge technology to make it incredibly fast; it also has very impressive facilities for the passengers: bars, lounges, and viewing platforms, as well as many shops and restaurants.

Cat-link V

Length:	91.3 m (300 ft)
Width:	26 m (85 ft)
Weight:	500 tonnes (550 tons)
Passengers:	800
Cars:	200

Flying boats

A peculiar way to speed across water is in a W.I.G. boat. W.I.G. stands for Wing In Ground-effect. These boats skim across the surface at high speeds. They are a kind of cross between a hovercraft and an aircraft. They travel at such high speeds because they do not touch the surface of the water. There is no drag effect to slow the craft down.

The Caspian Sea Monster

One of the first W.I.G. boats was an Ekranoplan, which is Russian for "screen plane". It was nearly 100 metres (328 feet) long and could carry 1,000 soldiers. It weighed 540 tonnes and could reach speeds of 563 kilometres an hour (350 miles per hour). To create the speed needed to lift it from the water surface, this Ekranoplan had 10 jet engines. It became known as the Caspian Sea Monster because of its awesome size.

Scientists and engineers have tried to perfect W.I.G. boat technology for many years. There have been many experiments and **prototypes**, but no one has got it quite right … yet.

The Pelican Ultra

The aircraft manufacturers Boeing are working with W.I.G. technology on a boat known as the Pelican Ultra. Even though it will fly like a normal aircraft, the Pelican's main function will be as a W.I.G. boat. The idea is to build craft much faster than normal transport ships, but much cheaper to run than aircraft.

✂ Make the connection

Wing In Ground-effect: the theory

Just before an aircraft touches down, it suddenly feels like it does not want to go lower. This is due to the air that is trapped between the wing and the runway, which forms an air cushion. W.I.G. boats use technology to allow them to ride on this cushion of air.

>> What is the future?

The armed forces are very interested in Boeing's plans. Military forces have to move heavy equipment as quickly as possible. The Pelican would be able to carry seventeen of the world's largest tanks at amazingly high speeds.

The Pelican Ultra is being designed to carry huge amounts of cargo over vast distances, skimming about 6 metres (20 feet) above the ocean. It would have a **wingspan** of 150 metres (492 feet) and a **fuselage** longer than a football pitch. It would dwarf all existing aircraft built for carrying heavy loads, including the world's largest aircraft of today.

Boeing hope that the Pelican Ultra will be the future of transporting cargo. Will huge container ships become a relic of the past?

The Pelican would take off from ordinary airports, using 38 landing gears. It would have 76 tyres to carry its weight. It could carry up to 1,400 tonnes of cargo. Boeing believe that only large transport ships can rival what the Pelican could carry, but at nowhere near the same speed.

If Boeing does manage to make the Pelican successful, transport of cargo on water will be changed forever.

Super subs

If you were sitting in a luxury jet zooming over the ocean, it would be difficult to imagine anyone travelling more quickly. Little would you know that a few kilometres down under the sea, a slim, grey, pencil-shaped craft is speeding past you. Yes, it is a **supersonic** submarine.

The supersonic submarine – fact or fiction?

No one has actually built a supersonic submarine yet, but the technology to make one certainly exists.

The technology for a supersonic sub began as a Russian experiment to improve the speed and accuracy of torpedoes. Any object, no matter how **streamlined**, suffers **resistance** as it moves. For example, you can feel air resistance against your face when cycling quickly. As water is about 1,000 times as **dense** as air, 1,000 times as much drag is felt. The Russians wanted to find a way to overcome the dragging effect of the water: the answer they discovered was bubble power!

They designed a torpedo called the Shkval. This produces a high-pressure stream of bubbles from its nose and skin. These coat the torpedo in a thin layer of gas to form an "envelope" of bubbles around the shell. This reduces **friction** and allows the torpedo to travel at much faster speeds. In fact, this torpedo could travel several times faster than anything else underwater.

✕ Make the connection

Surface speed

By 2008, the FastShip will be poised to break all records for the speed of surface ships. A new ship design with a wider **stern** is being built. FastShip's hull shape makes it lift up at the back, letting it move very fast indeed. Special engines suck in water and then blast it out of the back. It is thought that the FastShip will be at least twice as fast as the most advanced ships today.

Underwater travel – what is the future?

US scientists built on the technology of the Shkval. In fact, they have made it look slow! In 1997, researchers announced that they had broken the sound barrier … underwater! They used specially designed bullets and the bubble technology to record amazingly high speeds.

Even though objects can now travel underwater at incredible speeds, there are still problems to overcome before a supersonic sub becomes a reality:

- Power source: so far, the high speeds have only been possible over short distances. A form of power must be developed that creates enough energy but is still small and light.
- Steering: so far, anything using the bubble technology can only travel in a straight line. If there is something in the way … hard luck!

However, scientists are convinced that high-speed underwater travel is the long-distance travel of the future.

Some scientists argue that high-speed underwater travel will be more environmentally friendly: engine fumes will not be released into the atmosphere.

Train technology

Trains are very good at travelling quickly in straight lines. But what happens when the track is very curvy? Ordinary trains have to slow down and time is lost.

Tilting trains

Tilting trains have special upper sections that can be tilted sideways. In a curve to the left, the train tilts to the left to compensate for the centrifugal push to the right (see box below). This allows tilting trains to travel much faster on normal tracks.

The APT

In the 1970s, a tilting train called the Advanced Passenger Train (APT) was developed in Great Britain. Unfortunately, the project had many problems and was never successful.

The technology was taken over by an Italian company named Pendolino. They produced the Class 390. Over 50 Class 390 trains are now being used in Great Britain.

The new trains run at around 200 kilometres an hour (125 miles per hour), although top speeds of over 225 kilometres (140 miles per hour) are possible.

The TGV

The TGV is France's *Train à Grande Vitesse*, or "High-speed train". It is one of the fastest conventional trains in the world. Under test conditions, the TGV has reached speeds of 515.3 kilometres an hour (320 miles per hour), setting a world record in 1990. The TGV runs on special tracks at very high speeds, but it

✂ Make the connection

Tilting and centrifugal force

When a vehicle goes round a bend at speed, a force called centrifugal force pushes back against the vehicle. The force stops the vehicle from travelling as quickly as it does in a straight line. This is what causes packages to slide about, for people in chairs to feel pressed against the armrest, and standing passengers to lose their balance.

Some vehicles can easily compensate for this centrifugal force. Some vehicles and bikes simply tilt over towards the direction of the bend, allowing them to go much faster. Normal cars or trains are unable to do this.

can also operate just as well on ordinary tracks too. This gives the TGV an advantage over other high-speed trains, as money does not have to be spent on special exclusive tracks.

However, normal signals by the side of the track would be useless for the TGV; the train travels too quickly for the driver to see them properly. Signalling is done by electrical pulses through the rails. These give instructions directly to the train driver.

Stylish, sleek, sophisticated, and spacious: the motto of the TGV.

Marvellous Maglevs

"Maglev" is short for Magnetic Levitation. This means that the trains are designed to float just above special tracks, called "guideways". The trains use magnets instead of wheels. The main difference between a maglev train and an ordinary train is that maglevs do not have engines in the usual sense. Instead, electrified coils in the guideway walls produce a **magnetic field**.

Engineers claim that because maglevs can climb steeper gradients, they are environmentally friendly: fewer cuttings through the countryside are needed.

These fields **repel** large magnets that are underneath the train. This allows the train to rise above the guideway. Once the train has risen, it is moved along the guideway by adjusting the power to the coils.

Designers believe that maglev trains will eventually link cities that are large distances apart. At 500 kilometres an hour (310 miles per hour), you could travel from Paris to Rome in just over two hours.

Converting existing track will be hugely expensive. As there is 171,861 km of track in the UK alone, no one is likely to convert all of this into maglev track.

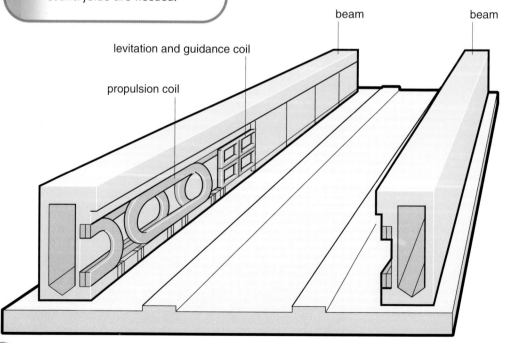

beam

beam

levitation and guidance coil

propulsion coil

✕ Make the connection

Maglev trains can reach very high speeds because they actually run above the track. The lack of friction and the trains' **aerodynamic** design allow maglev trains to reach awesome speeds of more than 500 kilometres an hour (310 miles per hour). A further advantage is that less maintenance is needed. Because the train floats along, there is no contact with the ground. This means components do not wear out. Finally, maglev trains are much quieter than conventional trains as there is no wheel noise.

The MLX01

A special 43-kilometre (27-mile) track in Japan, called the Yamanashi Line, is where the MLX01 is tested. ML stands for "Magnetic Levitation" and the X means "experimental".

In 2003, the MLX01 set a new speed record of 581 kilometres an hour (363 miles per hour), beating the TGV's old record. This shows that maglevs have the potential to travel much faster than ordinary trains. The MLX01 is also testing special safety features such as aerodynamic braking, should the magnetic systems fail.

There are some problems with maglev design. Building the guideways is much more expensive than normal track. As maglev trains can only run on guideways, the best option might be special high-speed routes connecting large cities. A solution could be to put normal steel wheels onto the bottom of a maglev train. This would allow it to run on normal track once it was off the floating guideway.

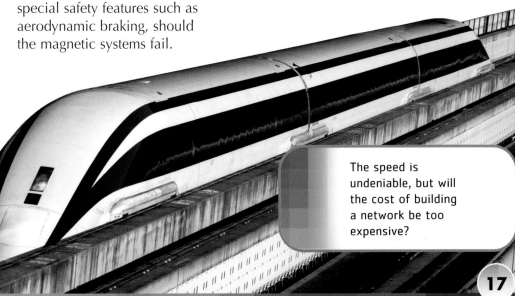

The speed is undeniable, but will the cost of building a network be too expensive?

Faster than a speeding bullet

If you want to ride on trains with cutting-edge technology, Japan is the place to go.

The Shinkansen

The Shinkansen, or bullet train, was the world's first high-speed train. Services started in 1964 with speeds of 200 kilometres an hour (124 miles per hour). Many countries, including the USA, still do not have any trains running at this speed. Instead of struggling with an old-fashioned train network like the rest of the world, the Japanese started from the beginning.

They "reinvented" the railway. If you consider that all of this was being built as British Railways were introducing their last steam locomotive, it helps to illustrate just how revolutionary their ideas were at the time. Many argue it was the success of the bullet train that led Europe to take an interest in making trains go fast.

"Shinkansen" actually translates as "new trunk line", but the term is commonly used to refer to the trains themselves.

Nowhere on Earth can you buy a normal train ticket and travel at such high speed as in Japan:
- Tokaido line: trains operate at 270 km/h (168 mph)
- Sanyo line: trains operate at 300 km/h (186 mph)
- Tohoku line: trains operate at 275 km/h (170 mph)
- Joetsu line: trains operate at 275 km/h (179 mph)
- Hokuriku line: trains operate at 260 km/h (162 mph)

The Shinkansen set the standard for high-speed rail travel. There is still nothing else in regular service to match it. There may be some trains that can go faster, but these are still experimental.

The Shinkansen remains the fastest train in regular service. There are, in fact, many of these trains operating all over Japan on special high-speed tracks.

The country's Shinkansen network has been developed over more than 35 years. It covers all main trunk routes. It will be a long time before other countries catch up.

Between Hiroshima and Kokura the bullet train covers the 192-kilometre (120-mile) distance in only 44 minutes. The train has an average speed of 262 kilometres an hour (164 miles per hour), making it the fastest scheduled train service in the world.

Safety not speed

Critics argue that high speeds should not be the main goal of a train service. Safety and passenger comfort are more important. Many high-speed trains can cause motion sickness, especially the tilting trains. Passengers have also complained of being pressed into their seats while going around high-speed bends in the track.

Taking the Tube

To beat the current speed records, new thinking is needed. An exciting development in the future could involve **vacuum** tubes. Maglev trains would run through these tubes at very high speeds. The trains would float on **super-conducting magnets**. But, because they are travelling through vacuum tubes, there would not be any air friction, and far less power would be required.

Super speed records

- Fastest conventional train: TGV-A (France) 515.3 km/h (320.2 mph)

- Fastest diesel-powered train: British Rail HST (UK) 238 km/h (147.8 mph)

- Fastest steam locomotive: *Mallard* (UK) 201 km/h (125 mph)

- Fastest **narrow-gauge** train: 6E electric locomotive (S. Africa) 245 km/h (152 mph)

- Fastest third-rail electric train: Wessex Electric (UK) 174 km/h (109 mph)

- Fastest maglev train: MLX01 maglev train (Japan) 581 km/h (361 mph)

- Fastest scheduled average speed between two station stops: Shinkansen 500 series between Hiroshima and Kokura (Japan), 261.8 km/h (164 mph)

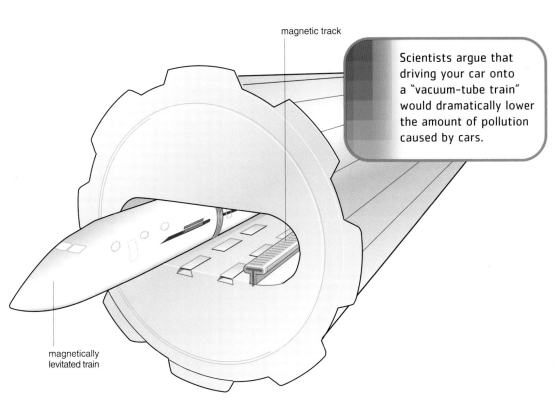

magnetic track

magnetically
levitated train

Scientists argue that driving your car onto a "vacuum-tube train" would dramatically lower the amount of pollution caused by cars.

The developers imagine the globe covered with a network of tubes. Each tube would contain a maglev train travelling at speeds of up to 3,700 kilometres an hour (2,300 miles per hour). They believe that such a system would become a serious rival to air travel. The only drawback would be the cost of building such a network of tubes, and the amount of time it would take to do so.

A similar idea also involves vacuum tubes together with your own car. The idea is that you would drive your car to the nearest transport terminal, board the train, and enjoy the ride. Each car would enter an individual compartment, large enough to drive your car straight into. The compartment would then shoot along a network of vacuum tubes to your destination and you then drive off.

A huge advantage of using vacuum tubes for transport is that they could go anywhere on Earth, even underground and beneath the sea.

Amazing motorbikes

For years, designers thought that the way to build the best, fastest motorbikes was to concentrate on the engine. Everyone thought "the bigger, the better". They did not consider that bigger engines needed bigger, heavier frames and fatter, chunkier wheels and tyres, which make a bike slower, not faster.

Less is more

Recent years have seen "the bigger, the better" idea fall away. Cutting-edge technology for motorbikes now concentrates on the idea that "less is more":

- There are now fewer separate parts. Instead of welding or bolting parts together, designers now create more complete parts, built as a single piece. This means less weight.

- Anything that has to be joined together is no longer welded. Super-strong glue is used.
- Lightweight metals, such as titanium and aluminium, are now used.
- Stronger plastics are used for the bodywork. This means they can be much thinner than before.
- Wheels have far fewer spokes, sometimes as few as three.

As the engines do not have to move such heavy weights, they do not have to be so huge to get maximum performance. Less weight means more speed.

The Fireblade

The Honda CBR 900RR Fireblade started the "less is more" concept. It was first built in 1992 and started a trend that all other manufacturers have copied. Honda has updated the design each year, and it is still a bestseller.

✕ Make the connection

Safety or speed?

Campaigners for road safety argue that many of today's motorbike designs are reckless and dangerous. They believe that the cutting-edge technology should only be in the hands of experts, not on ordinary roads. Since the mid-1960s, over 100,000 people have died riding motorbikes in the UK alone. The statistics show that bikers are 42 times more likely to be killed on the road than a car driver.

Suzuki GSX–R1000

Many experts think that this machine is the best bike on the road today, although the arguments will continue. Nevertheless, this Suzuki is lighter, quicker, more compact, and simpler to handle than most other bikes. It has the most advanced **engine-control electronics** available. Even the exhaust gases are extremely low.

The Tornado

Another contender for the title of world's best bike would be the Benelli Tornado Novecento. It has an unusual design as the radiator is actually under the seat. This makes the bike more stable. The Tornado has also been voted the world's best-looking motorbike.

The Benelli Tornado *Novecento*. Beauty and power without doubt: but should such a high performance bike only be allowed in the hands of experts on a race-track?

The beast!

Riding motorbikes can be a thrilling experience. Many bikers are looking for the ultimate high-powered ride. They need look no further than the Dodge Tomahawk.

By any standards, the Tomahawk is an extraordinary machine. It started life as an experiment, but there are now plans to build special orders to go on sale.

The incredible appearance of the Dodge Tomahawk is only the beginning. It has four wheels. It has an engine bigger than some military tanks. It accelerates like a bullet from a gun and has a mind-boggling top speed of around 644 kilometres an hour (400 miles per hour).

When seeing the Tomahawk for the first time, most people's reactions are "Wow!" and "Why?"

A bike for engine-lovers. What better way to showcase an engine?

The Dodge

The Tomahawk started life as a **concept car**. Dodge is a company that does not build motorbikes, but is famous for designing exceptional cars, such as the Viper.

The Dodge Tomahawk

Engine size:	V10 – 8277 cubic centimetres
Top speed:	approx. 644 km/h (400 mph)
Acceleration:	0-100 km/h (0-60 mph) 2.5 seconds
Power:	500 **bhp**
Engine speed:	6,000 **rpm**
Overall length:	259 cm (102 inches (in))
Overall width:	70 cm (28 in)
Overall height:	94 cm (37 in)
Seat height:	74 cm (29 in)
Weight:	680 kg (1,500 lbs)
Ground clearance:	7.5 cm (3 in)
Fuel tank capacity:	12.3 litres (3 gallons)

The biggest problem for the Tomahawk designers to overcome was the power of the engine in a motorbike's frame: the solution was to build a bike with four wheels! Each pair of wheels is very close together, in the same way that large lorries have twin wheels to carry the massive weight.

The Tomahawk is a reminder that cutting-edge technology is not simply about the fastest or the most powerful. It is about the "WOW!" factor too.

✕ Make the connection

When asked about exactly why Dodge had produced such an extraordinary machine, they replied, "It demonstrates how our designers are not bound by conventional thinking." The designers believed that no one ever sat down and analysed something to a very high level and came up with a great invention. They argue that great inventions are often simply a crazy idea ... but with hard work they are sometimes not that crazy.

Super scooters

In recent years, scooters have come back into fashion. They are cheap to run, easy to ride, and great for getting around cities full of traffic.

Honda Silver Wing

This super scooter is powerful and has many luxury features. In fact, it is easy to mistake it for a motorbike. It has a powerful engine and can go at speeds of over 177 kilometres an hour (110 miles per hour). It also has a large storage area beneath the seat and is as comfortable to ride as any other two-wheeler. The makers call it a scooter with attitude: the point where scooter and motorbike meet.

BMW C1

Is this the safest two-wheeler on the road? The scooter with a roof was laughed at as a gimmick when it first went on show, but the C1's excellent safety technology is no longer sneered at. The roof is part of a steel frame that protects the rider more effectively than anything else on two wheels. In crash tests, it did better than many small cars. It also comes equipped with seatbelts, and designers are currently testing a version with front and side airbags. It even keeps you dry in the rain.

The Silver Wing is similar in style to its famous cousin: the Honda Goldwing motorbike.

SILVER WING

Environmentally friendly

Much of the cutting-edge research that is being done with two-wheeled transport is not concerned with "bigger" or "faster". The research is all about "cleaner" and being more environmentally friendly.

Two wheels have an advantage over four wheels in this respect. Scooters use very little fuel. But it is in terms of **congestion** that bikes really come out on top for those worried about the environment.

Roads are becoming increasingly crowded, which leads to a range of problems:

- delays
- frustration and anger
- minor accidents or incidents now cause significant difficulties
- employers estimate that billions of pounds are lost every year to delays caused by congestion.

Everyone agrees that there should be fewer vehicles on the road ... but only if *their* car or bike is allowed to stay.

>> What is the future?

Bikes are best?

A dramatic increase in bike sales has coincided with increasing congestion. Many travellers are discovering that it is quicker and cheaper to get around on two wheels. Bikes can avoid traffic queues by squeezing through them; they can go where cars cannot. But what about comfort? And poor weather? These are reasons that put people off converting to two wheels. Perhaps the future will see development of vehicles such as BMW's C1, a "car" on two wheels.

Pedal power

Cycling has been both a popular sport and a simple means of transport for many years. But it was the 1984 Los Angeles Olympic Games that saw a real change in bike design.

Carbon–fibre technology

In the Los Angeles Games, the spokeless, super-light **carbon-fibre** disc wheel was first used.

Another revolution occurred in the 1992 Barcelona Games, where Great Britain's Chris Boardman won his country's first cycling gold medal since 1920.

Boardman broke world records and lapped the world champion in the final. His bike used carbon-fibre technology and aerodynamic cross-sections. It weighed less than 9 kilograms (20 pounds).

Since then the bikes have got even better. They are even lighter, stronger, and quicker.

The Brompton

Another bike at the cutting edge is the Brompton, but in a very different way. The Brompton is a bike that rides well, is safe, and yet folds easily into a compact and portable package. It can be unfolded in around 10 seconds and is very light. This means that you could take it into the movies and park it in the seat next to you. You could even park it under your desk at work. If you got tired when out riding, you might even want to get a taxi and sit with the bike on the seat!

Carbon-fibre technology is now becoming standard on many ordinary bicycles.

Balancing act

The Segway Human Transporter (HT) is a unique means of getting around. There is nothing else like it. You simply step on board, and off you go.

This unusual device gives you the ability to move faster and carry more, so you can travel, shop, and run errands more quickly and efficiently. It is also great fun to ride.

The Transporter looks like it will overbalance at any second. But this machine contains amazing cutting-edge technology. This means that it always balances itself.

The HT is also environmentally friendly. It runs on electricity and does not give off fumes. You simply plug it into a plug socket, charge it up, and off you go.

✕ Make the connection

The concept of the Segway works in a similar way to our own sense of balance. We all have inner ears, eyes, muscles, and a brain to keep us balanced. The Segway HT has several **gyroscopes**, tilt **sensors**, high-speed **microprocessors**, and powerful electric motors working to keep it balanced. These systems continually make tiny adjustments, 100 times every second. The balance will always be perfect whether you are carrying loads, travelling quickly, or standing still.

Dream cars

Road cars

How should we judge the most amazing car for use on normal roads? Should it be the fastest? The most powerful? The most expensive or luxurious?

The Bugatti Veyron

Whatever your own personal opinion might be, the Bugatti Veyron would be very difficult to beat.

This monster has more power than a **Formula 1** racing car and currently holds the world record for acceleration speed. If that is not enough, the car is actually electronically limited to 400 kilometres an hour (248 miles per hour). If this restriction was removed, an extra 100 kilometres an hour (62 miles per hour) would be possible.

Inside, the driver is surrounded by leather; even on the floors and the roof! The car has the most expensive music system ever fitted in a car and has every electronic gadget you can imagine. Many car experts really believe that the Bugatti Veyron is as good as it is possible to get. To create a car much faster will require adding even more weight and delivering even more power to the wheels. Many agree that you could not get much better than the Veyron in terms of performance from a road car.

Bugatti Veyron

Top speed:	400+ km/h (250+ mph)
Engine:	7,993 cubic centimetres
Gears:	7
0–100 km/h (0-60 mph):	2.9 seconds (world record)
0–300 km/h (0-180 mph):	14 seconds
Price:	approx US$1.5 million

Ferrari Enzo

Top speed:	350 km/h (217 mph)
Engine:	6.0 litre V-12
0-100 km/h (0-60 mph):	3.3 seconds
Height:	114.8 cm (46 in)
Cost:	US$652,000

Ferrari Enzo

Another contender for the title of Greatest Road Car is the Ferrari Enzo. It is named after the company's founder, Enzo Ferrari. Only 400 cars have been built. And that is it! When Ferrari make a **limited edition**, they really mean it!

It is not enough just to be rich if you want to own an Enzo: you have to apply to Ferrari for the privilege of owning one. If you are lucky enough to be accepted, the price includes a visit to the company's main factory in Italy to have the seats and pedals specially designed to fit you.

Ferrari have created a **street-legal** Formula 1 car. The critical thinking behind the design was to produce a racing machine that can be used on ordinary roads. The steering and gear systems are the same as those driven by the world's top Formula 1 drivers. The **chassis** is super light and the interior is not crammed with luxuries. Apart from air-bags, air-conditioning, and leather seats, the enormous cost of this machine pays for a pure driving experience.

The a.d. Tramontana

The startling beauty and total luxury of the a.d. Tramontana will not be easy to match. Only twelve will be produced each year as it is a far from typical sports car. The cars are completely handmade and only contain materials of the highest quality. All the parts are produced individually by skilled craftsmen, without the use of robotic machinery and mass-production.

Each car will be unique. While a customer's car is being built, they will be able to choose from a great range of **custom features**, such as having the engine and chassis inscribed with their name. The driver is also measured to make sure that the car fits perfectly.

The car has safety features as good as those on professional racing cars. Most of the body is made from carbon-fibre. The highest quality aluminium used to build jets is also present. Inside, only the finest materials are used, such as gold, stainless steel, and the highest-quality hardwoods.

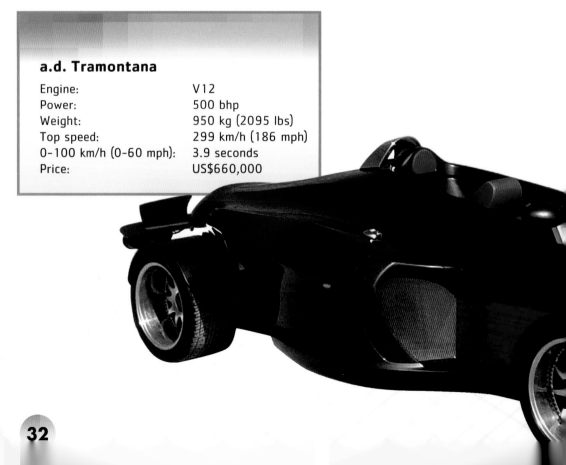

a.d. Tramontana

Engine:	V12
Power:	500 bhp
Weight:	950 kg (2095 lbs)
Top speed:	299 km/h (186 mph)
0-100 km/h (0-60 mph):	3.9 seconds
Price:	US$660,000

Pininfarina Birdcage Concept

This supercar is completely unique in its appearance. The body is divided into two halves. The upper section is transparent; the lower portion acts as the structural "skirt". The upper area offers amazing all-round visibility for the driver. It also allows many of the mechanical engine parts to be seen. The designers believe that engines are under-appreciated. So, they want to make sure that their beautifully crafted V12 engine can be appreciated.

The car stands only a metre high and is extremely aerodynamic. It is no coincidence that the car looks similar to some race cars of the 1950s and 1960s, as the designers

Pininfarina Birdcage

Engine:	V12
Power:	700 bhp
Weight:	1,500 kg (3308 lbs)
Length:	4.65 m (15 ft)
Width:	2.02 m (6.63 ft)
Height:	1.09 m (3.58 ft)

based the car on road-racers from this period. In particular, the car looks like a futuristic version of the great Maserati race cars of yesteryear.

The car has a transparent **heads-up display** instead of a standard instruments panel. This is similar technology to that used in fighter jets, and means the driver does not have to look away from the road.

Powering the future

Most new research into road vehicles is not concerned with speed or performance. The cutting-edge technology is developing new sources of fuel. This is not only to help keep the planet cleaner, but because there is a limited amount of oil on Earth – one day it will run out.

Electric cars

From the outside, an electric car looks just like any other. But you would notice a big difference when driving: an electric car is virtually silent. Under the hood, there are a lot of differences too:

- The petrol engine is replaced by an electric motor.
- The electric motor gets power from a **controller**.
- The controller gets power from rechargeable batteries.

Much work is being done to develop electric cars that run on rechargeable batteries. Although an electric car can be charged from an ordinary plug socket at home, the process still takes ten to twelve hours. Specialist chargers can do the job more quickly, however, in around five hours. Electric cars also have to improve their range, as they are limited to travelling only 80 to 160 kilometres (50 to 100 miles) before a recharge is needed.

Many lease and hire companies are keen on electric cars. Large businesses are also using them as "company cars" because they are so economical around busy cities.

>> What is the future?

The problems with battery technology explain why there is so much excitement about the latest development – fuel cells. Fuel cells are smaller, much lighter, and are instantly rechargeable. When fuel cells use hydrogen, they do not produce the environmentally damaging gases produced by petrol. The cars of the future will probably be electric, getting their power from a fuel cell.

e.Volution

The e.Volution is a vehicle that is powered by fresh air! It is being predicted that the e.Volution will be able to travel up to 200 kilometres (120 miles) for around 16 pence. This vehicle could revolutionize travelling in cities.

The engine is powered by the release of **compressed air** that is stored in tanks under the car. The car's body weighs only 700 kilograms (1,544 lbs), and the engine itself is a mere 35 kilograms (77 lbs). An engine driven by compressed air offers enormous benefits to the car designer. Because of its small size and weight, many normal parts are no longer required. The designer is free to use materials and space more economically.

The designers of e.Volution say that to refuel, it will be possible to simply plug the vehicle into any electrical power source to fill it up. This will take around four hours. The vehicle will run for up to ten hours at an average speed of 80 kilometres an hour (50 miles per hour). The makers hope that air stations will become as common as petrol stations, where a fill-up may take as little as three minutes.

The exhaust "fumes" are totally pure and completely safe to breathe.

From windmills to motor cars: quite an achievement for fresh air!

GM AUTOnomy

If the car was invented today rather than a century ago, what would be done differently?

This was the simple concept behind the AUTOnomy, built by General Motors. This car is set to redefine the way cars are built, designed, and powered today.

AUTOnomy is the first vehicle designed around a fuel-cell propulsion system. It is also the first to combine fuel cells with computer technology. This allows steering, braking, and other vehicle systems to be controlled electronically rather than mechanically. Driving one of these vehicles would be more like playing a computer game.

The car body does not need a traditional design. Drivers do not have to sit in the traditional place. They could move to the middle of the vehicle, or they could move much closer to the front bumper, or further back. There are no foot pedals or steering column. The body shape could therefore be anything you want it to be.

The makers believe customers will buy a chassis, and then buy different body shapes to put on top. These could be swapped about as the user needs them. The body of a ten-seater minibus could be very simply swapped for the body of a sleek sports car or family saloon.

Instead of buying a whole car, why not simply buy a new body-shape to drop over the chassis?

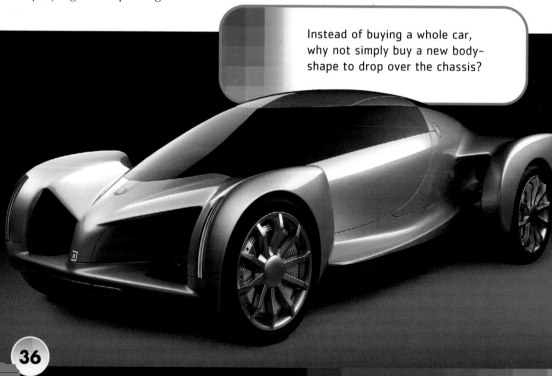

Safety

Vehicle safety has always been an issue. Thousands of people die in motor vehicle accidents each year. In recent years, car makers have realized that customers do not just want high speeds and great performance – they want a vehicle that is as safe as possible.

>> What is the future?

The introduction of seat belts, air-bags, and steel safety cells has helped to improve safety, but what does the future hold? These new ideas could be standard features in a few years:

- Several designers have developed an in-car breath alcohol testing system. Before the car will start, the driver has to prove they are fit to drive or the car will not start.
- Nissan have developed a Drowsiness Warning System. A small camera analyses driver blinking rates. As a driver becomes sleepy, blinks become longer and more frequent. The system warns the driver and sprays air-freshener into the car.
- **Cruise controls** are being designed that automatically keep you a safe distance from other cars.
- Just like aircraft, some cars have "black boxes". These record information about accidents, which allows designers to make improvements in the future.
- We are used to air-bags ... but all around us? Research is being carried out on vehicles that have air-bags completely surrounding the driver, even on the floor and roof!

The Toyota Personal Mobility (PM) concept car

Another direction for the future of the car is the Toyota PM. Because people spend so long isolated in their cars, Toyota has designed a vehicle that encourages drivers to join together in a mobile community.

The driver of a PM is able to communicate with other PM users. To share the burden of driving, several PMs can team up in a follow-the-leader arrangement. One PM becomes the lead vehicle, while others follow on **autopilot**. Each of the following vehicles has an on-board computer that controls that car, and keeps a safe distance from other PMs in front or behind.

The lead PM driver is in charge of direction and speed. Toyota believes that this feature will allow a new form of car-sharing. People familiar with an area could show short cuts to others. Of course, the system also allows a driver to relax and rest while another PM does the work.

The Toyota PM looks a little like a flightless helicopter on wheels. The driver steps through a front hatch as there are no side doors. As the PM moves, the cabin can tilt to allow the driver to sit in a more relaxed position.

Toyota's vision of the future encourages "car sharing" while still in your own vehicle.

The Alessandro Volta proves that electric cars can still have awesome looks and fabulous performance.

Alessandro Volta

To prove that environmentally friendly cars can also have great looks, power, and performance, Toyota have designed the Alessandro Volta. The car is named after Alessandro Volta, who invented the electric battery in 1800.

This car is a hybrid, which means it has more than one source of power. The car can use normal petrol, but it also has batteries that allow it to run off electricity. The Volta is powered by a V6 engine plus an electric motor on each axle. The engine provides 408 horsepower and allows the car to travel 700 kilometres (435 miles) on a 51.86-litre (14 gallon) tank.

Toyota have shown that hybrid technology can be used in a high-performance vehicle. The Volta can go from 0 to 100 kilometres an hour (60 miles per hour) in 4 seconds and reach a top speed of 249 kilometres an hour (155 miles per hour). It could not keep up with a Ferrari but it is still very quick. It uses much less petrol too.

The Volta can seat three people side by side. There are not any mechanical systems either: a computer turns the wheels, activates the brakes, and carries out all other functions. The driver uses an electronic hand-controller. This system allows the driver to operate the car from any position inside.

Highways of the future

There is little point in having cars, lorries, and bikes with cutting-edge technology if the roads are so crammed that no one can move. The average US motorist spends 36 hours a year standing still in traffic delays. Large sums of money are being spent in developing devices to ease the traffic nightmare. Highways of the future will need to be just as "cutting edge" as the vehicles themselves.

Pay as you drive

This idea is not new. Sometimes drivers have to pay to cross certain bridges or enter certain cities. But this often means having to queue at a kiosk to hand over the money. In the future, all vehicles may be fitted with special sensors. These sensors will send a signal to receivers at the side of the road or will be monitored by satellites. A central computer will then work out where the car has been and how far it has travelled. A bill is then sent to the car owner.

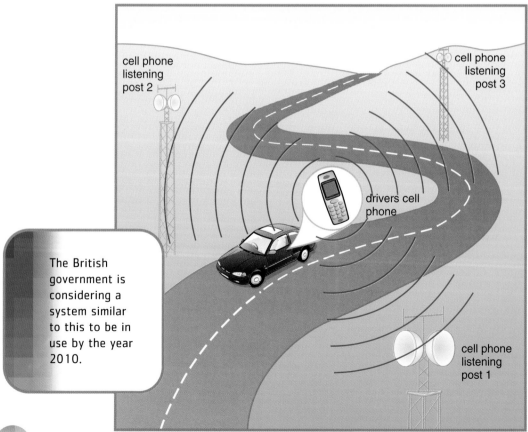

cell phone listening post 2

cell phone listening post 3

drivers cell phone

cell phone listening post 1

The British government is considering a system similar to this to be in use by the year 2010.

Mobile phone technology

A problem with intelligent highways is the cost. Installing receivers would be very expensive. Another plan is to tackle traffic problems using technology that already exists: mobile phones.

Many people own a mobile telephone, and thousands more customers sign up every day. There are plans to use this existing technology as part of an advanced system for managing roads.

Listening posts that detect signals from mobile phones are put up. Once three listening posts detect the same phone signal a central computer takes over.

The computer can quickly calculate the vehicle's location and speed. A message can then be sent directly to the mobile phone warning the driver of delays ahead. If the car has a **satellite navigation system**, a quicker route can be suggested and a map displayed on the car's system.

A right to privacy?

Many drivers are concerned about privacy. Tracking systems such as the ones described here mean that the location of a car is always known. It would be almost impossible to travel undetected. Is it right that our movements are always being watched?

✂ Make the connection

The same sensors and receivers used for payments could be used for a range of different things. One plan is to monitor the speeds that vehicles are travelling. When a roadside receiver detects someone travelling too fast, a signal could be sent to the car that would automatically make it slow down. This would mean that speed limits could not be broken.

Awesome aircraft

Passenger planes

For years, the world's largest passenger jet was the Boeing 747, the "Jumbo Jet". Now, the Airbus A380 has taken over as the biggest.

The A380

The Airbus A380 is huge. It has two passenger decks that are the widest ever built. Every passenger will have more legroom, and the seats are wider than any others. The lower deck has sleeper cabins, lounges, special rooms for business meetings, and even a crèche. Some A380s may even have a gym on board. The first-class area is more like a hotel lounge, passengers can move around and even have a drink at the bar.

The A380 uses the most advanced technology available. It is also the most fuel-efficient and the most environmentally friendly jet ever built. It takes only 3 litres (less than a tenth of a gallon) of fuel to transport each passenger 100 kilometres (62 miles). As well as this, a lot of effort has gone into making the engines quieter than ever before.

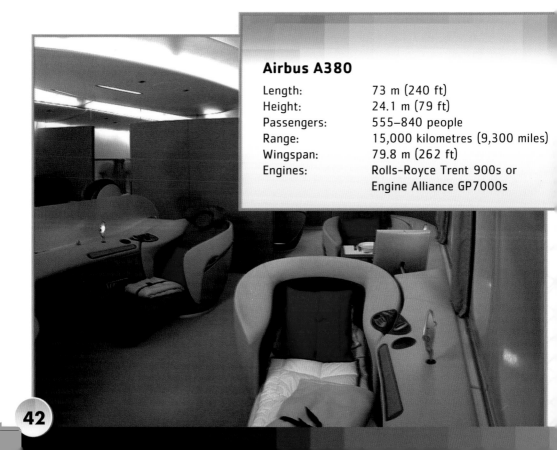

Airbus A380

Length:	73 m (240 ft)
Height:	24.1 m (79 ft)
Passengers:	555–840 people
Range:	15,000 kilometres (9,300 miles)
Wingspan:	79.8 m (262 ft)
Engines:	Rolls-Royce Trent 900s or Engine Alliance GP7000s

Antonov An-225

Engines:	Six Lotarev D-18T turbofans
Max payload (internal or external):	250,000 kg (551,250 lbs)
Wingspan:	88.4 m (290 ft)
Length:	84 m (276 ft)
Speed:	800 km/h (500 mph)
Height:	18.1 m (60 ft)

Cargo planes

It is not only people who need transport. Without cargo planes there would be large changes to our lives, particularly with regard to what we eat. There would be no more bananas or kiwi fruit in the winter; it would all be rotten by the time it reached us by road.

Cargo planes are the real monsters of the air. They are much bigger than the planes we use to go on holiday. The biggest of them all is the Antonov An-225, the largest plane ever to fly.

Antonov An-225

Known as "Mriya", the Antonov An-225 can carry a monstrous amount of cargo inside it. But its carrying capacity does not stop there. Mriya was specially designed to carry "piggy-back" loads that are too big to fit inside. It can even carry a space shuttle on its back.

This aircraft also has the most up-to-date technology for loading. If the cargo is not spread evenly through the aircraft, take-off can be very dangerous. All loading aboard Mriya is computer-controlled.

The X-planes

X-planes are behind all the new cutting-edge technology of aircraft. The X stands for experimental. The single purpose of the X-planes is to test new ideas. Without X-planes there would be no supersonic jets, **stealth aircraft**, or space shuttles. In fact, there would be no jets at all.

Some X-planes are built to try out new engine designs. Others have been built to test amazing speeds or to fly at very high altitudes. X-planes usually look quite strange and futuristic. How they look is not important though, as the planes only exist to carry out experiments.

X-43

The X-43 is an X-plane that is still being developed. It is intended to test designs for the first "hypersonic" aircraft. Hypersonic means that the aircraft will be able to travel above **Mach** 5 (five times the speed of sound). The designers hope that the X-43 will eventually travel at Mach 10, which is around 11,580 kilometres an hour (7,200 miles per hour) or 3 kilometres (2 miles) a second!

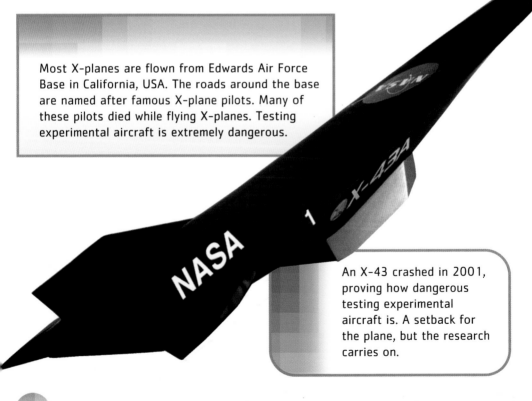

Most X-planes are flown from Edwards Air Force Base in California, USA. The roads around the base are named after famous X-plane pilots. Many of these pilots died while flying X-planes. Testing experimental aircraft is extremely dangerous.

An X-43 crashed in 2001, proving how dangerous testing experimental aircraft is. A setback for the plane, but the research carries on.

Aircraft pollution – the debate

Not everyone is happy with air transport. Some people claim it causes too much pollution and damages people's health. There are two main areas for concern.

Noise

For those people living close to airports, or underneath a busy flight-path, life is very noisy. Apart from damage to hearing, such noise can cause lack of sleep, irritability, heartburn, indigestion, ulcers, high blood pressure, and possibly heart disease. The sound of a jumbo jet taking off, heard from 600 metres (1968 feet) away, is around the same noise level as a car horn being blown right next to your ear!

Air pollution

When a jet takes off, toxic gases are released and spread over an area extending many miles all around. It is claimed that the areas around airports are very heavily contaminated. A study done in Chicago, USA, claimed that as many as 5 million people could be affected by a single airport.

✂ Make the connection

Aircraft are responsible for over half of the pollution caused by transportation. There are surprisingly few aircraft in comparison to the many millions of vehicles on the ground. Each aircraft must therefore release massive amounts of pollution. For example, a jumbo jet taking off causes as much pollution as 2.4 million petrol lawnmowers all operating at the same time.

Private jets

If you are lucky enough to be very wealthy, you could afford to buy a private jet. This means you can travel anywhere at top speed, and not just when a flight is available from an airport.

The Gulfstream G550

Private jets are very luxurious – almost like small hotels in the sky. The Gulfstream G550 is incredibly luxurious and extremely expensive. It is also the most technologically advanced private aircraft in the world.

The Gulfstream G550 is able to fly at altitudes up to 15,544 metres (51,000 feet) and at speeds of over 1000 kilometres an hour (620 miles per hour). It can fly eight passengers and four crew members 12,500 kilometres (7767 miles) the longest range available in a business jet. In effect, this jet can fly direct from New York as far as Tokyo in 14 hours. It can also take off and land from short airfields. This means that the owner can choose many more places to visit.

Flying at the cutting edge does not come cheap though. You can expect to pay around US$50 million for the pleasure of this jet as your means of transport.

Where on Earth would you like to go today? Provided you have the money of course!

Airforce 1

Crew:	26
Passengers:	76
Model:	Boeing 747-200B
Engines:	General Electric CF6-80C2B1
Range:	12,552 kilometres (7,800 miles)

Airforce 1

Airforce 1 is a specially designed and built Boeing 747. It is the personal plane of the president of the United States, so it could be called the ultimate private jet. Not only does it transport the president all over the world, it also has many special features. In an emergency, the president could run his entire country from the air.

Accommodation for the president includes an executive suite that consists of a stateroom (with a dressing room, lavatory, and shower) and the president's office. A luxurious conference and dining room is also available for the president, his family, and staff. Other separate accommodations are provided for guests, senior staff, Secret Service and security personnel, and the news media.

Because Airforce 1 is such an advanced plane, many call it "the flying White House".

>< Make the connection

Airforce 1 has cutting-edge anti-missile technology. It even has a shield to protect against a nuclear blast disrupting the electronic systems. It also has the most advanced navigation systems available. The plane's communications system provides worldwide secure communications. The equipment includes 85 telephones, as well as multi-frequency radios for air-to-air, air-to-ground, and satellite communications.

Race to space

In the past, using a rocket was the only way to travel in space. But these rockets could only be used once and were very expensive. What was needed was something that could be launched like a rocket but would land like an aircraft, so that it could be used again.

The space shuttle

After years of design, construction, and testing came the Orbiter, nicknamed the space shuttle. The Orbiter looks similar to an ordinary plane. It is shot into space attached to rocket boosters and a large fuel tank. Once the craft is high enough, the boosters and fuel

Lifting the 2.05 million kg (2,050 ton) shuttle into orbit requires around 2 million litres (530,000 gallons) of fuel.

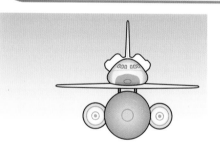

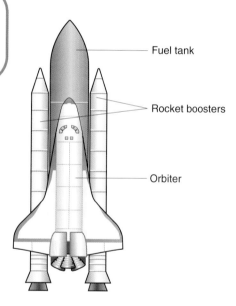

Fuel tank

Rocket boosters

Orbiter

Launch: the engines are ignited and the rocket takes off.

Rocket booster separation: two minutes after launching, at a height of 45 km, the boosters fall away and float back to Earth by parachute.

Fuel tank separation: 99 minutes after launch the fuel is used up. The fuel tank separates, falls back to Earth, and burns up on re-entry.

Orbit: the Orbiter carries out its mission.

⤬ **Make the connection**

Many believe that the enormous amount of money spent on developing space travel could be better used by improving things on Earth. They also argue that space travel is too dangerous. By 2004, around 100 people had died as a result of accidents while developing space travel. The best-known of these is the explosion of space shuttle *Challenger*, shortly after lift-off in 1986.

tank fall away, and the Orbiter carries out its mission in space. The Orbiter then re-enters the Earth's atmosphere and flies back to Earth, landing like a normal aircraft.

The shuttle has four main parts: the Orbiter, a fuel tank, and two rocket boosters. Apart from the fuel tank, these parts can be used many times. But scientists are in search of a craft that is 100 percent reusable.

A US$10 million dollar prize was recently won by a team that built and launched a fully reusable rocket. This can blast three humans into a sub-orbital flight (100 kilometres or 60 miles high) on two consecutive occasions within two weeks.

The space shuttle Columbia crashed, in 2003, while attempting to land. Heat protection tiles were damaged and the craft broke up 61 km (38 miles) above Texas, USA.

Space planes

There are a number of ideas being tested to make the space plane a reality. Currently there are several experimental X-plane models (see pages 44–45) in development that could make space travel as common as jet plane travel. Many people believe that space could soon become a holiday destination.

X–37

The X-37 looks a little like a mini version of the space shuttle. It is designed to test and improve the **thermal protection systems** that keep spacecraft from burning up during re-entry. The X-37 does not launch under its own power. It is carried into orbit on board the space shuttle. It travels at speeds of around 30,000 kilometres an hour (18,600 miles per hour).

X–34

This amazing craft tests many of the fuel options that scientists are experimenting with. It has already performed many tests in flight, attached to another aircraft. When released, it flies at around 10,000 kilometres an hour (6,200 miles per hour) and is able to glide into a landing on a regular airfield.

Bringing the cost down

For scientists, the biggest problem is getting into orbit cheaply. Despite the shuttle's many accomplishments, the fact remains that it is extremely expensive to launch into space. The cost of fuel for each launch is still awesome. The hope for the future lies with the radically designed X-33.

The X–33

The X-33 is a prototype for a unique straight-to-orbit craft. Its wedge shape is unlike any spacecraft design before. At its base, the X-33 is 23.5 metres (77 feet) wide, and the craft is 21 metres (69 feet) long.

This design allows the spacecraft to hold all the launch fuel on the ship itself. There is no need for rocket boosters or a huge fuel tank. Without these, the weight is greatly reduced and much less fuel is needed to get it into orbit. It is hoped that an X-33 launch will be ten times cheaper than today's shuttle launches.

There have been problems, however. The cost has already gone far past US$1 billion and the makers, Lockheed Martin, have not yet been successful in creating a material to build the fuel tank.

The ultimate goal of the X-33 is to produce a commercial aircraft called the VentureStar, a successor to the space shuttle. Not only could the VentureStar be used to put **payloads** into space, but it could also be used as a space tourism craft. When tourists first go into space, they will probably have the X-33 to thank.

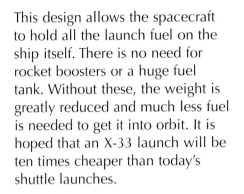

Will the X-33 lead to the first tourist space-ship?

Science fiction or science fact?

The idea of time travel has been around for centuries. It continues to fascinate us today. When Albert Einstein created his theory of special relativity, he also produced a strong argument for the possibility of time travel. Of course, no one has yet been able to travel in time … but no one has been able to rule it out either.

So, do the events of science fiction ever have a real chance of becoming science fact? Many writers have created ideas for time machines, but a real-life time machine has never been built. In fact, scientists believe a machine is unnecessary, as natural **phenomena** will transport us instantly from one point in time to another. The only problem is scientists are unsure if these phenomena actually exist!

Scientists are investigating whether there really could be some fact in science-fiction!

Black holes

These are huge stars that have burned all their fuel and are collapsing under their own weight. Incredibly strong fields of gravity suck everything towards the black hole, even light itself. A black hole is a little bit like an ice-cream cone. It has a large opening but tapers to a single point, known as the singularity. At the singularity, everything is completely crushed.

Some scientists believe that black holes could be used as doorways for time travel or travel to parallel universes. They argue that some kinds of black hole do not actually have a singularity, and we may be able to pass straight through them. This would be our way to enter other times or other worlds.

Wormholes

A favourite of science-fiction programmes, wormholes are believed to exist by many scientists. Not only could they allow us to travel through time, they could allow us to travel incredible distances from Earth, in only a fraction of the time it would take with ordinary methods of space travel. They are basically tunnels that connect different parts of the Universe.

It is believed that wormholes could provide transport in two ways. Firstly, they connect great distances, so distant places could be visited in a lifetime. They would also allow vehicles to travel at amazing speeds close to the speed of light. According to Einstein, that is when time travel becomes possible.

>> What is the future?

If time travel does become reality, we could produce very complicated problems called paradoxes. The most famous is the grandfather paradox. Imagine a time traveller went back and accidentally killed one of their grandparents before the traveller's parents were born. How could the traveller exist if their parents were never born?

Glossary

aerodynamic designed with a shape that will move easily through the air

autopilot device which guides a vehicle on a chosen course

bhp brake horse power – a standard measurement that compares engine power

carbon–fibre very strong, hard, but light material

chassis frame of a vehicle onto which the body is fixed. Normally including the wheels and engine.

compressed air air which has been squeezed into a small space

concept car car built to showcase an idea and not normally intended for mass production

congestion overcrowding

controller device that relays power to an electric motor

cruise control a system that maintains a vehicle at the same speed without the need for the driver to maintain it

custom feature specialized, unique feature of a vehicle

dense closely spaced, compact

drag any force acting against a moving object that slows it down

engine-control electronics computer signals that adjust the performance of an engine

foil "wing" beneath a ship that lifts it from the water

Formula 1 classification of racing car

friction force that slows things down when they rub together or move over each other

fuselage main body of an aircraft

gyroscope wheel that always remains steady when spinning inside a frame

heads–up display vehicle control dials that are projected onto the windscreen. The driver can still see the road through the screen and does not have to look away from the road.

hull part of a ship that floats on the water

knot unit for measuring the speed of ships. 1 knot = 1.85 km/h or 1.15 mph

lift upward force made by the air on an aeroplane wing or similar structure

limited edition when a restricted number of something is produced

Mach a measurement of speed. Mach 1 is the speed of sound, or 1,225 km/h (761 mph); Mach 2 is twice the speed of sound.

magnetic field force produced by a magnet

microprocessor part of a computer that controls its main operations

narrow–gauge railway track with a width of 1067mm between the rails

payload amount of goods or people a vehicle, such as an aircraft, can carry

phenomena event that can be observed, especially something rare and special

powerboat small racing boat with a powerful engine

propulsion act of driving forward

prototype first example of something, from which later versions are developed

repel push away

resistance force that slows a moving object

rpm revolutions per minute

satellite navigation system
technology that allows a car's position
to be pinpointed by satellite and
transferred to route maps on a display in
the car

sensor electronic device that receives
signals and acts upon them

stealth aircraft aircraft designed to be
difficult to detect, particularly by radar

stern back part of a ship or boat

streamlined designed to move easily
through air or water

street–legal vehicle that can travel
legally on normal roads

super–conducting magnet type of
electromagnet (magnetic field caused by
running electricity through a coiled wire)
where there is virtually no resistance to
the flow of electricity through the wire

supersonic faster than the speed of
sound

thermal protection system device to
prevent extreme-heat damage

vacuum enclosed space with all the air
and gases removed

V–hull boat with a hull that has a
V-shape to cut through the water

wingspan maximum distance across the
wings of an aircraft or bird, measured
from tip to tip

FURTHER RESOURCES

Mean Machines: Sports Cars, Chris
Oxlade, Raintree, 2004

Superbikes: The World's Greatest Bikes,
Alan Dowds, Book Sales, 2004

Designed for Success: Superboats, Ian
Graham, Heinemann Library, 2004

Mega Book of Aircraft, Lynne Gibbs, Neil
Morris, Chrysalis Childrens Books, 2004

Index